Printed in Great Britain
by Amazon

35729213R00056